www.finishinglinepress.com

Alphabet

poems by

Mara Jebsen

Finishing Line Press
Georgetown, Kentucky

Alphabet

ACKNOWLEDGMENTS

3quarksdaily: "A is for Ardor," "B is for Blight"
American Poetry Review: "Rogue," "Virgin"
fogged clarity: "C is for Chryse & Chrysanthemum," "D is for Deed," "E is for Easy
and F is for Fate"

Publisher: Leah Maines

Editor: Christen Kincaid

Cover Art: Mara Jebsen

Author Photo: Mara Jebsen

Cover Design: Elizabeth Maines

Printed in the USA on acid-free paper.
Order online: www.finishinglinepress.com
                   also available on amazon.com

Author inquiries and mail orders:
Finishing Line Press
P. O. Box 1626
Georgetown, Kentucky 40324
U. S. A.

Table of Contents

for Shabazz and all of the Clovers

"*Maybe in order to understand mankind, we have to look at the word itself. Mankind. Basically, it's made up of two separate words: "mank" and "ind". What do these words mean? It's a mystery, and that's why so is mankind.*"

—Jack Handey

A is for Ardor

Ardor is life.
Is the zeal in a line down the center
of the body.
The wick.
I *ascend*, with burning
eye. Ascend: to rise
over mountain
and lesser; to take on, in some sky
the space of dominion. Now
animated. Now moved
from within. Fully half
of all ancestors are women.
Their scrubbed faces, so hard
to know. The frame around mine,
and the frame around yours
could melt—there was a song:
my grandma and your
grandma,
        sitting by the fire-

but one tossed the other's flag
in the flames.

Now, now, our ancestors
are moving,
in circles, in skirts, in their different
houses. Let us will them:
Leave their houses!
Burn skirts together!
Ancestor worship
is veneration of those dead,
whose blood we believe
runs thread-like
through our own; blood that now
holds sway over we living.

Ahankara is the false
identification
of the true inner spirit
with the body,
or mind, or outside
world.

Which is to say?
It all
burns off,
except the wick,
the promise of fire.
Are we ardent spirits,
like brandy and gin?
I try to picture
myself without a body. Oh dear
grandmama, most inflammable
of flammables; here is how I know
you go dancing like blazes
in the waltz of the beyond:
when I spin,
I burn; hands open, receiving
the gust of a gift called ardor.

B is for Blight
a linguistic miseducation for belles

A balalaika is a Russian instrument with a neck
like a guitar. Not to be confused
with balabaika: to talk nonsense, faradiddles, hogwash.
Or balderdash (which is
of course
       bullshit, horseshit , but a quite a bit
       gentler—almost to babble
       like a babe.)

       It is important to know: a ball is a lavish, formal
       party. Where belles cluster
by balustrades. But a ballotade is a way a horse moves,
       drawing in the leg so the iron shoe shows.
Blackknot makes spots on cherries and plums.
       Blackleg attacks the thighs of goats.
 And sheeps.

Well, there can't be belles
if there aren't peasants. This is how one dances
in an age of plagues. Lets talk rot with our loving
baby's breath. Let us mixer betwixt
white columns & farces, masked balls, lame horses, whilst
black-hearted knaves
bear knives on highways. Lace me my corsets?
Damsels must be *protected*
from farmhands' handsy
gropes. With folded fans. With cordons. With ropes.

C is for Chryse & Chrysanthemum

chryselephantine: meaning
overlaid in ivory and gold—
chryse: a wealthy greek courtesan, whose maids bathed her
from clay pots with great sponges and smearings
of honey; who was bangled with gold, who offered
at Aphrodite's temple
nightly gifts of perfume—
chrysalis: a thing unformed
chrysolepic: some creature, let us say a dragon, or fish,
golden-scaled.
crisis: the turning point in a disease, which indicates recovery
or death.

this sound, "chrys," repeated often enough, takes us to a shore,
i think, & golden-scaled fish
swimming in pearly-blue water. a number of shells & eggs, harboring
formless things, which will culminate
as winged-bugs or as beautiful
women. a heart-attack
is a crisis of the heart—a death, or a healing in a flash like
the cracking
of a mysterious
egg.

D is for Deed

which we can picture arising from the mind of the woman from
The Yellow Wallpaper, perhaps long before the story begins

degrade defile de—

A deed is what is done by the doers; who are agents of what's
intelligent, responsible and do-able
in the universe. Doers: hold deeds
on parchment paper, to keep on holding
to the deeds   they've done. No one knows
what a death-candle is, but some have seen it
shimmer among mountains. to Deface is to mar
the features of a thing, even if that thing
is faceless, immaterial—

& in the dementia of the night, it is hard
to know
what's done or undone; you have
defaced my inner thoughts, i cried out
but you said: indeed? that's not possible.

E is for Easy and F is for Fate: Sheherazade in Love

A Fabricatress is a woman who Frames, who makes, who builds,
who constructs: a liar.
Something Fabulous is celebrated in Fable, a rare thing
that shimmers at the edge of belief . . .
Facile: easy, free from labor. To lift what pains the body and mind
Easy on the Eyes. Easy as Pie. Easy. Slut?
Facet: in diamonds, a multitude of Faces. In insects, any
of the small lenses
of a compound eye.

She's two-faced, sweet-faced, witty, facetious. Sheherazade is bug-eyed
and saying what she sees: a thousand versions of the same love story:
each one starry/ but brutal by the end. A film's cut down to a thousand
nighttime slices/ A thousand moons show a thousand trickster faces.
There's a thing that's false, but shiny in nature/ Sometimes its ok to
trust/ what's easy. A thread of something real/ twists through the
gossamer/ Don't hurt the spider.

Everybody Knows That a G is a Gangster

A G is a gangster or a thousand bucks, or
"what you use to call someone who you don't know like a cabby"
or a dude you like, who has his shit
together. It's a kid's letter, City letter,
slick, efficient: gluing up a genre of several spectral men:
friendly guy, ideal, and violent player "differentiated
by valence and circle of use."
Philadelphia. 1983. Albert M. Greenfield Public School
Class 3a (3rd graders) gathered together near the shining
oak planks of our school's best feature,
the intimidating auditorium, to enact a skit
called "Vocabulary Hospital." Jacinta and Kelly are roped
at the waist, and are giggling together,
as conjoined twins—Jacinta is "Give" and Kelly is "Me"
They stagger on stage, their voices commingling:

> Gimme Gimme Gimme!
> Is What The Children Shout!
> And Now We Don't Know Who We Are!
> Or What We're All About!

The doctor performs an incision. I got a fake
broken leg. Am a piteous martyr, the dropped
G, always left behind,
when the kids they go a-runnin' and a-laughin'
and a-jumpin.' I ham it up bigtime.
Then I get 'cured' and after the show, we all pronounce our G's
For maybe two minutes. It sounds so hokey
we dissolve in laughing heaps.

The Philadelphia official who gives a speech
on the worn planks of Greenfield's auditorium,
when we graduate, stuffed
in our new teeny bodies, dressed to the nines in nerves and white,
is not a G. He doesn't know *his* Shakespeare
could emit from such vessels. His eyes
go big like a shepherd who has heard the sheep speak.
His very astonishment
makes him stutter. The kid next to me mutters:
"gee-whiz, mutherfucker."

Hell As We Know It

is the punishment of the wicked
after death.
If I raise hell,
if you catch it—we go to it
in handbaskets.
Leander went swimming the Hellespont
for his love. When he sank, Hero
drowned herself in blue water. And the blue
heron always looks like he swam here
for a visit away from his hell-blue
pit. Then, heroin
being cousin to morphine,
makes euphoria & godlike prowess
makes the mortals
more immortal, or dead. Hocus-pocus! Hollow
halo O, hominid, ancestor
of us and of apes, we inherited your see-through
electrifiable bone-head; we're built
like a match; upright, skyward-bound.
Something there is
made us
   into lovers
      & addicts; we're built
to look up
  at heaven as it blows
    bubbles, bubbles, bubbles of blue lava
thru the tops of our clear
       monkey skulls.

I is Me.

All
Mouth. Vessel
Of English. One of several
Flute-like beings populating
A conquered land. There's a
Tongue-haint hovers over. A ghoul
Of garbled
Lords and peasants, who hail from rain-green
Elsewhere Hills. There's tongue-ghoul
Of sequoias, & Schuykills, canoes; I-tongue haunted by pop
& mom & jazz & banjo. I-tongue with a map
Of Africa on it, then sickly red stripe and a cracked
Union Jack. A globe's cross-stitched, overlaid on the sweet
& bitter territories of american
Tongues. So then I is for baby, because crooning baby, baby
Is the downdeepy-deepest of this deepermost I. I
With salt-sugar and bud-bloomed-to-blossom
Bloody and creamy, gardenia-crowded mouth, all
4 u. 4 u, baby, baby, the American love song;
Sung with all quantity of pain the singer's gritsy-got. Drawn
Darkly down from the throat's sugarbowl; from the gleaming
Starshine at the base of the gut. Never flagging; one note
Periodically true—
From the home of the "we?"
Most hungriest,
                            most brave.

J is for Jigger

J is for jigger. As in jigger of rum, which tilts, like niggardly,
On the edge of its skin, damned by the sins
Of sonic association. But guilty, too. Like jigaboo.
And jackass music, our old friend jazz. Jack
Of all trades, jack of spades. Oh jujube. In one version, the J came in
On feathers and chains, from faraway, from djembes and Jerusalem,
From a land of jack-o-lanterns, and jimminy-crickets—
And J is gorgeous, Jittery, jeweled. It knows, like none other,
How to jam. It jams with brother "b" often as it can, being big
As jumbos and generous as jambalayas. J is everyday. Is your cuppa
Joe. Some kinds of Jesus. J bled it all out and jimmied up,
Shining. It is the tenderest letter of the alphabet.

K is for Kiln

A broke heart.
Has feathers.
Has bones.
In it.
A choke heart.
Is where the bird.
Goes to die.
The mind-kiln.
Is where the sex.
And the killing.
Happen. Where the flame.
Licks the clay.
Dry.
The mind-kiln's
A hot oven.
A burning mind.
Gets broken.
The desert.
Lies. On its side.
Like a breathing
Belly. Like a sleeping
Dog. A broke heart
Stitches shut
Like an eye.

L is for Lalala

advice for the lightly lovelorn

Lollygag. Be lazybones.
Lark. Let the tongue
Luxuriate in its field. Let the limb slip all
Simple. The mind loll.
L is silly. You stick
Fingers in your ears and say la la la la and lust.
burns oddly in the lily. A body,
even old, unloved, laps
at any stream; is a marvel
in the bath. List pleasantly
with it-ness. Be soft. Swallow the loop.

Mama is Mammoth

Mamma is Mammoth
Mamma is Monolith.
Mamma is monster and marvel.
The only child
of a single Mother
knows a Monotheism
intimate as a breast.
To grow is wrenching.
Is march in deep Mourning.
One must address oneself
to the streaked
sunset. Salute
that Muchness. That Manifold,
That Many. The mutilated affections
Multicolored, split, multiply
in clouds, by moods; then
by hope hope hope. Is there love
in the Muchness? Could luck, could it crack
from up high, like tipped
buckets of coins,
a-clattering, a-clattering; love
like a great,
invisible Manna?

The Nth Time

And then I told N
Never, Never, Never, again.
We were back in the garden. Nails
rusted in the coffin. A willow
hulked above the graves. A willow
wept and dribbled pollen.
I longed for N to the nth degree
Sang nonsense songs in the key of N
No, No, for the Nth time, No
And then, then
It was Never, again.
We were back in the garden.
Astink, righteous and rot.
Newborns, mewling.
I tongued the dirt, for bloodfoam and marrow
N held my neck in my neck's own narrow.
Had done me no wrongs.
Was Reconstituted, sweet-wrinkled,
New-wet as a newt—for the nth
Time we were
back in the garden.
Astink, righteous and rot. And then, I told N
Let it be Never,
Never, Again.

(O is for O)

(the poetic one)
—without an h, unencumbered, orgasmic,
whole, mouth-silly, perfect in its circular-ludicrous
        purity.

P's and Q's (mind them)

perfect p and her backwards twin q.

p: i have been known, i suppose
to be precise and prissy. to pin my pins
to the proper pincushions.
to have fingertips like paper; to be pent up
and prim.
it isn't so perfect
being perfect, you know,
but its perfect
enough, which is *technically* impossible: enough
to make a perfectionist   nuts.
(p-nuts?)

Q: About P.

she's pent up and prim as a whistle.
she never pinches or pilfers or poots.
she's got perfect pitch and a head like a petunia.

and she's polite.
she says "I'd prefer. . ."
and people slump beneath her will, swooning.
power slips from her lips.
like invisible
soup.

(but *i* see it!)

my dreams are bloated
with puppet-heads
nodding on stems
backwards on their spines

i'm deficient, disquieting
a duck
bound in the wrong
direction; quartermoon of my sister
less than her double, like shadow.
less than silver next to gold.
odd. quiet, queer, quirky, I aM tHe cRaZy
In tHe qUiLt.

but here's a secret:
U likes me.

and i like u.
we have a weird little song
we make together
quaquaquaquaquaquaqua!
and when i'm grown?
I SHALL BE QUEEN

Rogue

I do not wish to be this elephant
plagued with cemeteries and a mind that holds
and holds, watertight, the layers of losses—
and nuzzles the earth to turn up what it turns
and sweeps at the earth with the grace of noses;
I do not relish this thickness, these feet
slung at the ankle with a leathery drape
which dust up and pack down in cyclical fever
the narrowing plots of survivable brush.
I do not wish
to be an un-tusked mother who whines,
who thins in the corners of her sons' eyes—
not noting the tweak in each, the rivulet
of current striking out, mutating, mutant—
not predicting that made hysterical by loss
an elephant goes rogue, rams a grey grief;
lumbers its heady mass into the village
becoming denatured, denatured and aroused
to spectacular, vengeful killing sprees
(its ears aflame, fanning, raw.) As if losing
species. As if the animal body proclaims:
I cannot be what I am having seen what I saw.

S is for Solstice

depending where you are, you might

1) eat a persimmon
2) kill a wren
3) kill a white, female, animal
4) kill a person
5) bathe with lemons
6) switch places with a noble or slave
7) wear a special hat
8) perform a 'wine miracle'
9) pray the sun back
10) orgy. . .
11) put butter on a doorknob
12) worship the goddess of fertility
       and sanity, who is riding far
       overhead, slipping between
       each winter
       star,
       in her sled of reindeer bones.

T the Tragic

T's horrid in its torpor;
terror, daring titan—T wears
a tornado like a flipped-up
skirt. T is not democratic, but shall tear,
rogue-like, kicking, burning, across
the globe. Will traumatize countries.
Will eat them, then fronds
feather & prickle in the corners
of T's mouth. T picks, like a lady
selecting tart cherries, a single
thin face to trounce. We have spent
our human hours
making T.
making more T.
telling tales around T.
lying about T.
Tip-toeing—
like little
elephants—tippling and nosing
the graves of their dead. We know
T titillates, but only
from afar. . .
Oh T, your scent
makes our eyes smart—
a petticoated Goliath, as yet
met no David; you are completely
supreme, with triumph
that's ghastly.
—in your trail, our faces tremble;
go smash with light.

U Loves Again

It was
p u liked first. P was
perfect. When
u followed her, the head
whitened like the inside
of a helium balloon—when u
and p got together after a fight,
making up, up, up—
u dizzied in some thin blue
heights. But once, u glimpsed q
feeding ducks
in a pond far
below.
Arms akimbo. A figure
mostly bone and ferocious
lancing, a figure clouded
in little tufts
of bread.   u dropped down.
The irregular fields spread
their scored and icy
greens wider and wider. Something
had happened to q, u thought,
and u thought, as usual
that u
could undo it;
u couldn't. The birds
collected. Q
started to sing; it was forlorn
and almost lovely—U kneeled
and joined in.

Virgin

Somewhere there's a forest, and oil from the first,
the first
the first
olive—somewhere there's a ball
of raw
clay, and wool that's not yet spun.
And everything shimmers at the brink of despoiling,
And everything matters because of what could be done.

Here come the settlers. Here come the conquerors.
Here come the clumsy-handed devotees. Let them
Find God in the sawed off
Teeth of the elephant.
Find God in unmapped space—Let them chart the sky
And invent a virgin. May they chase the trail
Of charming not-ness. May they learn and un-learn:
Cleanliness does not
rub off on what it touches. Spoils
only do as they say. A vessel is a vessel—it holds
what it holds. In green-blue-black sub-strata soils
every event in nonlinear time.

W is for Wine

The sun, with all those planets revolving around it and
dependent upon it, can still ripen a bunch of grapes as if
it had nothing else in the universe to do.
—Galileo

Double You, I like hours and weeks
without wine, and a room made of windows
and white light in streams,
and the grapes in the valley are swelling, and caught
inside each is a flesh fat with sugar and more
I don't care.
    I don't care.

In the red days, I, and both of you, double you
swam through red streets and up the red stairs
and watched the red films and laughed the red laughs
wasted with waste we always called joy
what was always a spiral
what was always a swirl
that rose up and sank down, and down.

Then, once, or often, the moon, the moon
like a seed from its skin, slipped-bang
on the floor
I cried like a monkey. The morning was trash.
Winter had happened without my noting,
the will, or whatever inside, was a blur.
    What is waste? Was I lost? Does an hour, or four
warped but warm-blooded slide into the nothing?
I half-slept while you whistled, double you, both of you
the wanter, the wanted,   I waited

The wine grapes ripen even now in the valley.
I live a thin life like a thread in a sheet.
What will say when I'm old, when I'm old?
Once, I was young, I fell into a well.
The water was red; almost swallowed me whole.
There's a wrong kind of hope. But I'm glad
grapes make wine—
because hands can't hold water, wishes, or time.

X Marks the Spot

X, unknown, unknowable
cross; god's mark. where two
roads meet, i love you
monsieur, mademoiselle, anonyme.
language to name myself by. when i am
in this country where we are all
x's. please, please, examine my head. those
lines, at some infinite point,
they do meet, they cross, it is there
i am lost. There where my life
enters yours and my language

My two eyes are x's, my mouth
too, an x, i sign my name by
the x, with an x, because i am
analphabet, because i know no
language to name myself by. when i am
in this country where we are all
x's. please, please, examine my head. those
entirely leaves my tongue. even
animals have such strange
encounters, fearful lock of eye, i, when
paths cross, infinitely mirrored

And Sometimes, Y

Yes. With the whole eyeball, unto the inner
                              pupil,
    the shyest of schoolgirls inside me says:
    Yes. Yes to airplanes and starving and the mountains of the mind.
  Yes to excess and losing; my yes to your yes.
If that's what it takes, world. Open. Do your best.
    I've written a lot of poems, and I've said a lot of prayers.
I've sung it out and danced it out and sweated all I could.
That joy you put inside me—I tried to put it back.
    I've even swum towards you,
when you moved through the night sky. You,
thing, you *it*, You *all*.
You *what* that I leap to
When I'm most what I am.
When I'm happy as a yam.
    And not frightened by your size.
    And not frightened by my time.
When my heart knows every single thing that it can.
Not always. Not forever
        and never
            for long
  But sometimes, and sometimes,
    yes.

Z is for Zebra, Zebroid, Zedonk

As the zookeeper and his wife slept—
a zebra broke
the donkey manger's fence
to heed the thing called ardor.

When they named
the newborn zebroid "Ippo"
the starker of the Italian Christians
decried the "abomination."
But the abomination,
—it was adorable. Ippo, slender wonder
 of faintly striped legs, that he spread
out to rest
in the Florentine sun.
In the pictures,
(which you can find on the web)
Papa Zebra looks unrepentant
as if he is saying: I do not understand
why you brought me here.
Mama Donkey nurses "normally."
Ippo, of course, is a sterile zedonk.
And last of his line. Fine.
Because somewhere
in the new world, in a small part
of Georgia,
another neglected zoo
went to seed. Now sweet-grass
licks the striped calves of Pippi,
fellow-freak, dear-sister
long-stockinged zedonk.
    Let's ask: why
should these rare things
  bring us to marvel? Its simpler to note
      all of them are just
  cousins to horses.

Note: Pippi got
her Daddy's
mouth.

She is standing in her stockings with the pride of mutts
She is mouthing to her mother in her big zebroid tongue
        She's the creature, like all of us, on the rocky quest,
            The result of celestial maniacs.

Mara Jebsen is a poet, essayist and performer raised in Philadelphia and in Lomé,Togo. She holds a B.A. in African and African American Studies from Duke University and an MFA from New York University. A 2009 New York Foundation for the Arts fellow, Mara currently teaches undergraduate writing at the Expository Writing Program and the Tisch school of Arts and Public Policy at New York University. *Alphabet* is her first chapbook.